AFTER
THE
FOX

AFTER THE FOX

TRAVIS CEBULA
& SARAH SUZOR

Black
Lawrence
Press

Black
Lawrence
Press

www.blacklawrence.com

Executive Editor: Diane Goettel
Book Design: Amy Freels
Cover Design: Alban Fischer

ISBN: 978-1-62557-912-6

Published 2014 by Black Lawrence Press.
Printed in the United States.

for Elizabeth Robinson

Neither dark nor light
is my true love.

—Robin Blaser, *Cups*

Contents

Night and Day draw near and greet one another as they pass the great threshold of bronze: and while the one is about to go down into the house, the other comes out at the door. And the house never holds them both within; but always one is without the house passing over the earth, while the other stays at home and waits until the time for her journeying …

—Hesiod, *Theogony*

Catch us the foxes,
the quick little foxes
that raid our vineyards
now, when the vines are in blossom.

—*The Song of Songs*

Nocturnal, when was the last time you slept the whole night through?

The last time I held a book and listened to the leather rain.

The last time the rain was steady. Like footsteps.
Like marching up these empty halls. Filled.

Footsteps and pages turning. And pages torn, dropped
one by one into an alley for passing birds and winter.

Birds or rats. Or birds. I can't tell
which. I can't tell who has wings.

These old pages are wings, and made of stretched
skin. Skin scraped with knives to near white.

Old pages are old, though. The thinnest in the wind.

So difficult to hold age or whiteness. So both and neither
land in the hands that grasped for them.

Neither land on land, either. But the sea.
There is always a sea. Close.
Or near close. Or near near.

I want to believe that. Yes, I need to hear it
in the curl of a paper shell. Say the sea is near
this open book. Say so again.

ONE

Atlantic

In other words,
the coastline.
In other words,
The Empire State Building.
In other words,
after the fox.

Dear Nocturnal,
have you jumped into the edge of the Atlantic?
Have you
forgotten me?

•

After the fox, see
the chase. Feel the theater.
A grasp at something
with a velvet waist.
An overcoat fails. In other words,
midtown. In other memories,
hands were held in place
by pearl bangles.

By starlight.
May I call you

Morning, Morning?
I would say "again."
But it's been said,
again, and better than
once. I did not jump.

Once, I did not know
you or your other
more comfortable shoes, then,
worn when you strode

dripping from the ermine sea.

I do not forget
what I owe. I do not
sleep on your account.

•

The chase is accounted for, Nocturnal;
the chase is no longer
your biggest problem.
These streets run north and south.
This island, you see, is narrow.
The problem is there's never
enough time to catch you.

And starlight?
It's not summer anymore.
In other words,
I haven't been to the sea.
In other words,
I haven't seen you for days.

Go on,
talk about all the memories
you have in your head.
Go ahead and make a joke.
I'll be here,
watching the sun light
the skyline, light
the tallest buildings,
one at a time.
In other words,
the chase is accounted for
but I don't sleep either.
Dear Nocturnal,
this island:
it's narrow.

•

You speak of narrow,
of this island. I would not dare to
joke about something so serious.
Because I'm talking about legs.
We can agree here
on the tallest, yes. And longer.
We can agree on haste. We
can agree
on December.

An overindulgence of black
leather seemed more comfortable
then, after the fox.
In other words, not erotic.
In other words,
neurotic. Talking,
time squared and
squared again until one hour became
four hours blown walking.
In other words,
crosstown. A tandem stagger
past buildings lit
from inside.

It's not a gaptooth summer.

Say the sun won't slide down
like a tongue licks glass canyons.
Say the sun is not really chasing,
either. Not at this pace.

Morning, do
you ever grow tired
of your narrow tracks
in concrete, or the white
stare always scorching your back?

•

One hour squared
is one hour,
and that's all.
And that's a fact.
But you're right about one thing:
say the sun won't slide down.
Say the sun is sick of the chase.
The chase is sick of the sun.
In other words, Nocturnal,
after the fox there are no tracks,
no tired eyes.
After the fact,
there are no apologies,
no jokes to be made.

Somewhere someone
is looking for you.
Sometimes the Atlantic cries.
Somewhere else I might be someone.
But I'm not,
seriously, I'm not.

If I could, I would speak like you.
But I can't, seriously.
When I say "once more"
I prefer to say "again."
So, again, how easy is it
for you to live with your decisions;
how easy is it
to stare at the sun.

•

Climbing is not easy.
Morning, again is
never easy. Nor is after,
and that's a fact. That's physics.
That's all. I'll never
apologize on your behalf.

Someone may be searching
for me. In other worlds,
someone may be looking
at the sky now or building
a castle from green glass.
But it is not me
by the breakwater crying.

Morning, it is not me
or the Atlantic who cries
after the fox.

Or a corrugated box.
There are a myriad yawning.
On other days a broken
sunrise could be called
a dawning. On other days a rest.
Today this gift is for someone

else.

I am trying, but I
have never stayed,
and never
seen the sun un-
obscured by clouds.

Again or ever.

In another language,
there will only be the gulls
to welcome you back
from waltzing.

•

Nocturnal, my slow dance
might just be your biggest problem.
Let's talk about fear, huh?
Let's talk about crossing Broadway at midnight.
Remember?
You were always so good at remembering.
Stone or stare,
hunting or hunted:
let's talk about the way we moved
in moonlight.

Nocturnal, my slow dance
might be the stick
that breaks your back.
In other language:
après le petit renard,
in other words,
small animals can be sneaky.

In this city
there are only three things
you can be certain of,
one of which is fear.
Again and again.
Let's think about it, huh.
Let's duck in the alley,
break a bottle, and
talk about what each other
lack.

Remember? You were always so good
at finding those hidden places.

Nocturnal, you were always so sneaky.
What has changed?
What is it, exactly, that makes you
so scared?

•

I remember midnight.
There was never a reason to cross Broadway.
So why be scared? Why now?
There's no reason to leave.
Alleys are a quiet little —. Why
be scared?

I'll tell you. I'll sell you
my memories for the right price.
When did you abandon
the straight shot? Before this abnormal
dark, I remember moonlight
and waiting for fear
to clot. And you were there,
Morning, by the park,
with the broken glass and puddles.
The yellow cab. The streetlamp
bent horizontal. The shoe
like a small animal. Its cave.
Empty. There was a hidden place.
For once a barefoot fox.

When the dance stopped there was you, gloating
about how you only ever get started
at midnight. How you don't quit. How this city never
sleeps. Oh, Morning. Not with the sun.
That wasn't dancing. It was a seizure under red
and blue lights. It was a sheet
pulled up too high. It was the wet
on the street.

One wheel squeaked.
And that's the stick that broke me.

I agree with fear. I agree with three,
wherever they're strung.
The stone, the stare, the hunt.
I've been hung from too many poles
to crawl back. I bury all the old regrets
with you. I hold all those stark moments.

I hold the hands as they grow cold.
Just like you asked.

•

You don't agree.
Nocturnal, there is always a dance.

In this city
the second thing you can be certain of
is regret.
Go on,
talk about all the hands you've held.
All the lessons you've learned.
All the streets. All the slick, slick streets.
But don't tell me you've buried
anything.

My biggest regret,
ever or again,
is believing you.

I don't drink cognac. Remember?
And ladies never hail cabs.
Neon and streetlamps mean nothing
in the light of the sunrise.
Build me a fire, will you?
There is always water.
Don't you see the bridges?
Don't you know why they're there?

Don't you see,
this city is just like you.
And you are just like me,
inversed.
At least I admit my tender opposite.
At least I admit the dance.

In other words, Nocturnal,
I know the difference between

what is alive and what is buried.
I hear the cries. I hear the heart beat.
Barefoot for the first or last time,
let's talk about the things that haunt us.
In other words,
let's talk about the consequences.

In any case,
even in another language,
what's done is done, so
"why" doesn't matter.
It's always afterthought,
it's a streetlamp at sunrise.

•

The third certainty is I will follow you.
I will admit you when you knock.
Don't you see?

After thought, there sits only darkness.
We will finally arrive in one city
where we will be alike:
opposites, and tender.
There is no sun there, no cab,
no red neon fading to smoke.

No one will call sewer steam
beautiful there, even if it is honest,
even if its neck is fragile and so unlike
whatever else we've stolen. I admit now
when we stop to pick up coins
we hear all the hearts beat.
Even our own.
We both see holes

through people. You can't deny
I remember a bare shoulder or being so tired
I had to finish the cognac,
watching your back as you danced.
And you can't deny I rarely dance.
But that was my cognac. I held it in my cold hand.
I shouldn't have to tell you.
In other words, that wasn't the first.

I don't regret the last chance tango, the come and go.
The full rooms, the sublime trance, or
the city inversed so the rain
fell on the inside. Just like you
rehearsed. Morning, I believe

there is always an ocean
around us, even now.
I can hear its shell. I believe
in the consequences of regret,
I believe in you. I believe in your wet feet
and the next step.

Guess exactly what I want from you, and in return
I'll make it so you can only die once.

•

Oh your wish,
your last request:
selling remembered thoughts to
a quiet street corner?
Hoping and hoping the evening never ends,
rolls itself right back around?

I had a wish once.
I wrote it down and set it on fire.
I crossed Broadway and never looked back.
I needed heat.
Hasn't the city taught you about heat,
Nocturnal; haven't you set me free?

In other words,
inverse.
In other words,
consequence.
In other language,
every action has an equal
and opposite reaction.

Every promise creates a
tender and honest
expectation.

Every false moon houses
a scared and
barefoot fox.

In other words, you're not telling me anything
I don't already know.

I don't care whose drink it was.
I don't care if you ordered fourteen more.

I care about the consequences,
about the reaction,
about the way your feet hit the street that night.
Alone, Nocturnal.
We were both,
ever, again and still
alone.
But go ahead,
tell me about the wishes in the world.

•

It's not a corner
I wish for.

I wish for that time I forgot
to dread you.

We were twenty-two and it.
And it was almost dawn.
The arms of the trees were stark
against the sky in the only
park that mattered. We were central.

Remember the after-show glow
and how we both wore eyeliner?
We loved being dark. Fourteen
more or the whole
bottle, I wish I could pour
all that distilled amber onto autumn's
grass, drop a match,
and burn a patch of the world back
again. A black circle inversed
to then.

Remember how the early sun
flattered you?

We grasped hands. We ran
so fast no one could have
told us apart or told us from
the moon. No one could have told us
it was shining, or about heat, or
anything, or needed to.

We knew wet grass
only made sense barefoot.
What more did we need?

Sometimes, Morning,
barefoot only makes sense once.
Sometimes the consequence can't be matched.

•

I anticipated you would say that,
in other words,
I expected.
The question isn't plural.
Isn't we, but I.
What more did I need?

On these streets,
the third thing you can be certain of
is scarcity.
Nocturnal, it's everywhere.
After the fox,
I'd like to know your intentions.
Like to sit down and look you in the eye.
Either one.

Once and then we were young.
Is that what you're saying?
If so, you are wrong.
Dawn belongs to me.
Remember? That's the deal we made.
Split the park right down the middle.
Me: the Hudson,
you: the East River,
and all the scarcities in between.
Spit and shake on it,
that's the only hand-holding
I recall.

And still you wonder,
what more did we need?
I'll make you a list
while you sit there, writing down your wishes,
waiting for magic to burn a patch of the world back.
No, that was a good one.

Go ahead, wait for it.
Might as well eat your own arm.
Scarcity,
cross my heart, Nocturnal,
it's everywhere.

•

Anticipate me at the end
of every fading day. I'm the only one
you'll see. Scarcity is what's up.
That's a fact. That's a question of potability.
The Hudson and the East, those rivers ferment.
Those wet slivers rise
like yeast. An island splits the between.
And Nocturnal. And Morning.
And how the young ones fit,
how we're all so eager to be seen. So difficult.

You especially. That was the deal.

Sure I sit here, and recall
our seal, and how to keep the dawn
pure. We were all young once. We chose.
We froze our partitioned
hours. A small curse of flowers:
even if you're sure they're there, I recall
the young can't be
anticipated. On that we'll spit and shake.

Dream them back again by daylight. Take me there, I dare you.
Dream Us in that alley instead of I.
I'm not talking about innocence.
And we're too old for counting.

Scarcity is just the surface.
It's the little things mounting.
Underneath there's a labyrinth.
Below this city is a hollow
wide enough to swallow all of us.
I saw it swallow a train like it swallows piss.
It ate the fox whole, it ate the rain, and I went in
after it. Darkness is not plural,
it's just everywhere. Like spent hate.

The persistence of these streets is a miracle.
Expectations are all
that holds Broadway up.

I'd rather cross your heart
than it.

•

The only things under this island are
consequence, darkness and water.
Wet garbage, dead flowers, they float, they
never ferment.

But you sure crossed something:
your fingers.
Your cold, cold fingers.

Nocturnal, were you scared of the chase?
Humor me for just one second.
One second squared.
One second too long.

In other words,
I recycle this light out of obligation.
Call it innocence. Call
attention to my purity. My
intention.

Nocturnal,
I intend to fake it all the time,
even when I'm scared.

Remember that record you used to play?
And that view from your roof?
All the way to Brooklyn, yeah?
All the way.

•

What do you plan
to wear under that shadow gown?
In your gleaming
arms I see your sleeveless past.
But infrastructure is about arrival,
and from up here, the rooftops have begun to lie.

Under the tar-square mosaic the rain whips
sidewalks into snakes. Umbrellas crawl.
Every scale has its own
scrawled direction. All of the colors,
all of the lacks, shine.

Morning, if you arrive you will arrive
by bridge or by tunnel, in darkness. In slow dawning
dread or alive in cable-striped light.
You will come to it. And it will be a concrete
realization. And it will be
sudden bright. The city will rise
to block the sky. Blue or grey.
Or red fire.

I say you will own it all.
I say these will be your
clouds of granite.
In other words,
I give the odd streets to you.
Five and seven.
I give you a song of long jackets.
Heaven.

The chase is yours, for now.
Fake or not. After the river,
the fox looked so small.
So small beside such a tall bridge.

This revision of scale and
this perception,
this height—it's the city's
boldest correction. This flattened hulk?

It's also its cleanest bus, stopped only and just for you.

•

Nocturnal, I can only assume you mean what you say.
I can only say I assume.
We can agree on the broadest,
always, but the darkest, never.

I have been listening to the city's secrets.
I have been writing them down in the rain.
Do you have anything you want to tell me?

Remember that bar.
The one with the rules written above the toilet:
"No dancing."
"No name-dropping."
You could only assume I had read them.
You could only assume that's why I didn't.
But you were wrong.

Nocturnal, after the fox
there are four ways to get home.
There are five liquors to put in that drink.
There are 48 blocks that separate me from the park.
Half of which are even.

But in this city
there is only one person with your name,
and one person with mine.

Everyday I am delivered.
The question is not one of arrival,
but instead, one of departure.
If you leave, you leave forever.
So the question is not one of departure,
but instead, one of return.

Have you anything to say about coming back?
I'll buy the next round.
I can only assume you'd choose cognac.
But, I can only say I can assume.

•

Morning, you're in it.
From where I sit, it's only
safe to watch. It's too dark
and full of angles for me
to participate. But I'll tell you
a secret.

You talk about returning?
If you ask, Morning, you'll get
directions. You'll get five liquors and a train.
You'll get the A, the C, the E.
You'll get the R, the 6, the Z.
And if you hurry you'll get the uptown.
If not, you'll get the F.

The F is fine. If you like that.
It's no secret, but it's no cognac, either.
It's where I live when I'm here.

The candles are open
flames and they, too, are fine.
They are for touching
to paper and they are
for all the other deadly heat
that so many hands pass through
without noticing. In other words,
once the building caught fire it kept burning.
In other words, beautiful. And stranger than.

After the fox, I assumed
you'd be back. Forever
is a circle with four ways
to its edge. Dawn and sunset.
Noon and midnight in
days after days. We could be anywhere,

but I guess there's only one
Morning, and one Nocturnal.
Those are the only names we drop.
And so I repeat what you've said.
I repeat the rain and the rules.
It's no vain secret how to walk
around. It's no secret
how to be serious. I watch. I listen. I wait.

•

We could be anywhere.
But we're not.
We're in the middle of some serious secret.
We're in the middle of some secret street.
We're crossing at sunrise.
In other words,
constantly the middle.

And the buildings are made of bricks.
Nocturnal, do bricks burn?

It wasn't me who lit the match
but I was the one to blow it out.
I don't remember how I got there
or how I left.
All I know
is that it was serious.

I assume you say what you mean.
In other words,
fire only leaves ashes
no matter how lonely you are,
or which train you take.

Are you lonely, Nocturnal?
Is that what you're trying to tell me.

Lonely is only an empty sidewalk,
an empty bed,
a sad song with no one to play it to.
And empty is just that.
In other words, weightless.
In other words, quiet.
In other words,
after the fire there was no sound.

I don't know how you got there
or how you left.
I don't know what secrets you still have in your head.
All I can assume is that you knew what you were doing,
and you meant what you said.

Did you watch me
watching the flames die?
Did you watch me
watching the sky grow constantly more empty,
constantly more middle.
In other words, Nocturnal,
do you watch me?

•

Watching is serious.
But you know that.
You know the empty middle.
We could find it anywhere.

This city stands, vertical
between winters,
and when it burns, it burns
a shiver down. A candle
fizzles into the Hudson.
A shoe. Another and another.
Every dawn I imagine
the city sinking into you.
Like watching so much
confetti disappear into a New
Year. Light into a river of ash.

Anywhere the gash of night never ends.
Anywhere a jackal laughs
over a pyre of street signs,
and the sidewalk is empty—
somewhat less than a fox
because it is
dancing circles without music.
Because no sad song exists
in silent fire.
The sad songs they save

behind an unmarked door,
stashed in a jazz basement.

It's no secret, Morning,
It's only November.
It's only leaves crossing
avenues in the wind.

I am lonely, and
who wouldn't be?
I've felt no caresses,

I haven't spoken
to the sun for days.

The West Village is fading
into grey wool and black
dresses. In other words,
winter. Its dead leaves are ready
to burn. Aren't we all.

Constantly.

I know
you don't carry matches.
You're always asking
for a light. I don't blame you
or I for the smoke that lingers
in an otherwise featureless sky.

I watched the feckless
embers soar. After the fire
I watched the sun
to see if it would burn
a silent silhouette of your face
into the red
bricks of my living room wall.

In other words,
after the fire we both watched
the world go home alone.

TWO

After the Fox

How simple would it be to replace light with the memory of light?

How simple would it be to replace you with the memory of you.
You, with the memory of night.

> *To find a tight spot between buildings so narrow.*

How simple would it be to forget?

> *So high they'd hobble a day down to half.*
> *A few minutes.*

Now, three sighs and a song.

> *Plate glass to plate glass.*

A sign.

> *Three sighs with not-quite-open eyes.*
> *To make a pass, a hooded stare and just enough*
> *to abandon the sun for good.*

A direction.

> *To look at only one red spot all night.*

Crossed-eyes. Oh, surely there's space,
some tired place with an old wooden door and candlelight.

> *Sever it from the long hot fade to blue.*

No doubt, it will burn.

> *How simple would it be for me to burn you*
> *into a memory of you?*

No doubt, it will be the easiest thing the world.

> *How lovely. If ever or if every night.*
> *A memory of you could almost be a replacement.*

But perhaps there is no other fate worth facing.

> *There's no question of goodbye*
> *any more than there's a question of the sun.*

No figure better to replace than silhouettes.

> *Even when I'm blind drunk I'm still breathing,*
> *even with my eyes closed.*

Or shadows. Or any thing that only exists because of a flame.

> *And I see forty stars and more*
> *expressions on your face than I can count.*
> *And those will never go away.*

You are as blind as you are lost.
And you are as lost as I am.

> *I cannot say the candle will gutter to smoke.*

Saying goodbye is actually easy.

> *But perhaps that will be our fate.*

Two syllables and a knotted throat.

> *And perhaps is the easiest way*
> *to end a long night.*

But the million minutes of without?

                                    Sitting together
                        in a joint that doesn't allow dancing.

You count, I'll make a joke.
How serious would it be to replace you
with the conclusion of you.

                                    Save something for later.

You can run, right?

                        Save yourself a swing, and I'll grant you
                                a trapeze. Gracious or graceful,

Am I?

                        when you wear yourself out on the town—

Am I right where I said I'd stay?

                        when you heel-toe on the high-wire you shine.

If yes, how quickly could you come.

                        You meet midnight like satin on fire. You're right.

If no,

                                You're right where I left you.

then know, too many minutes are two too many.

Whereas something topples from your open hand,
whereas summer stops—

I have two hopes and three-thousand questions.

fire only moves one direction.

How serious is fire when the lights go out.

It keeps going up.

How necessary.

And light seeps out from the middle
of snowstorms.

How strange.

It keeps flowing.

The sound of heat.

It keeps us warm.

The sound of feet

So raise normal to no and a glass to yes.

clawing a tight rope.
No, I don't want to remember you this way.

I hope.

And, yes, there's always a chance to climb down.

Right before darkness I can trust me.

Hand under hand.

Right before too late I'll realize

There's always ground.

a dark window is a mirror. I'll realize my own face, and I won't blink.

Whereas the summer breeds simplicity,

I can't.

it's never the other way around. I hope you're right.

I think I won't miss the underside of this table for anything.

I hope, right before you're right, it turns into winter.

Its dark belly.

Into weather enough we have to run from door to door.

I won't miss my odd fall, or the right ride despite my melt slipping down. I'll even catch your glass, if I'm able.

I hope people think we're confused, crazy, lost.

I'll ease its landing with my teeth.

Displaced, not replaced.

Maybe bequeath you a drop.

No, it'd be too serious

The second one.

to come to any other end.

From under the table I'll be brave.

Too much of not enough.

Tell you to draw your own mask.

Not ever enough.

In other words,

Not enough of something drastic,

your own conclusions.

something worth chasing. I said: You can run, right? Am I?

THREE

Pacific

Morning, let's tip
the continent in your favor.
Make a commitment
to let it all roll downhill.
In other words, let gravity do
the work for a change.

Downplay. In other words, let's play
your game for a while.
Let's play the music loud.
Just because
I want the windows rolled down.
Just because I want the wind
to eat my hair. I want to get burned
by the sky. Just once,

I want to drive all the way west
into the ocean and drown—
watch the sun dip like Icarus
spit into a vat of melted wax.
I want to watch the world bloom red
right before the lights turn.

Because eventually all lights turn green.
In other words, be patient.
I know you have
110 ways of saying yes,
and I have 405 of no. So,
convince me there's more there than just
windows to distinguish tall buildings
from beaches. Sell me on it.

Say the right word
and I'll swap my black jacket
for a tin tub of ice cubes

and little crowns.
I'll throw all my wool down
on a pile of driftwood and broken doors.
I'll light a fire for a warmer night.

•

Look at you,
wishing for wind,
wishing for water,
wishing we weren't born binaries.
I'll let you believe it
because I want to.
Because there's nothing left to lose
anymore.

In other words,
I'll go conditionally.
I'll go crazy.
But I won't go committed.

Westward it is.

I know what happens in California.
I'll tell you all the way there.
I'll put my feet on the dashboard
and sing till I fall asleep.
Not never, but always.
Not if, but....

When we slide into the sea
promise you won't follow me,
you won't try to calm me down.
Promise you'll never watch me suffer.

You look like a stranger,
like something I can't recognize anymore.
Anymore, always or never.
Like all the stars in the sky.

Promise we'll see them
there, Nocturnal.
Not if, but when.

•

So there's nothing left
to lose. All the constellations
have been etched into sidewalks.
Footprints harden and nothing
is left for the sky. The rest is just talk. The rest is west.
You know what I know
about California? It's big.
Tectonic.

Westward. Huh. My wagon's a hearse.
I'm using dead
reckoning. So it's all about the looking, then.
It's all about when. As for wishing, well,
wishing for wind
will give you a handful of breath.
At most, a wish for water will fill your lungs

with sea. Who cares? When I go crazy, too,
I'll go whole-on, wish-we-were-never-born-crazy, oh, and binary
won't even roll into it. Believe it. Believe my stare.
Because if you believe you were never meant
to be born you'll never wish.
If you're never born you'll never die.
But never isn't the same as when.

Or why. I won't calm you down.
I won't even try. Until then, I'll just go crazy conditionally,
from heat and the glare off water.

Look how the fan of palm fronds bows to you.
Pretend it's a kiss.
I promise you if we both fall asleep
before we reach the edge of the world,
the water will wake us. The waves will take us into
their cold arms like strangers

coming home. *They will whisper seven times.*
Seven times and their hospitality will give us back

to the stars. If we go
we go together.
In other words, we'll go down singing.
When we inhale for the final
chorus, we'll drown.

•

Nocturnal, I'm gone.
The wind started singing to the sun.
In other words, the wind started singing to me.
Put another way, I'll meet you there.

It's the slowest death,
the longest stare,
waiting for you to come through.
It's throw-the-plate-across-the-kitchen.
It's cry-till-you-can't-open-your-eyes.
It's spit-in-the-wind.
It's putting-wishes-in-one-hand-and-shit-in-the-other
crazy.
Flat out crazy.

Forget the fronds,
I'm halfway through South Dakota,
and it isn't warm, yet.
Every mile west the moon gets softer
and a little more sad.
Every mile south something gets harder to swallow.
In other words,
if I'm not dead
I must be numb.
So if you come, you'll come alone.
You'll come carrying a box full
of promises.
In other words,
you'll come heavy.

Remember,
you were always so good at covering my tracks,
as scared as a rabbit,
but as fast as a fox.

In others words, Nocturnal,
I believe
you'll know where to find me.

•

You say you're gone.
It's the same slip of paper, the same sad story,
it's been the same for more
hours than I can count.
It's the same damn empty
box of failing daylight.
It's the same oily ounce of rain,
and its residue on my cheek feels like
chasing you my whole life, like chasing iridescence.
Sometimes west. Sometimes south.

I covered your tracks again, one at a
time back to the ocean.
It's been choking you for years, you know,
coating your throat numb from salt
water and a glass of other words
harder to swallow.

If you're not dead, it's before noon
and you're still driving.
You're diving into South Dakota,
swishing through stalks of fox-
tail grass. If you're up to something—
up to your eyes in it, say—
well, then, some part of me is, too.

At least you have the road.
At least you have California to pray to.
In other words, at least you have a black line
laid out in front for you to follow. All I've got
is a dusty memory of sunshine and, someday, the interstate.
When I wind myself up into that highway,
I won't turn. I'll burn the candle
from its center out. I'll twist the spring up tight.

Not if, but when,
I find that red note you stuck on the door—
I'll grind my heavy sole into the floormat.
In other words, my right foot
will never lift. One pedal and the wind strong as
the best song you've ever heard about death.

In other words, if you have to
wait, it might not be for long.

•

I'll wait
but I won't sit still.
When you arrive
it'll become a different matter.
A different conversation.
A matter of difference.

I can't tell you the truth
about the time in between.
You don't want to know what I'm up to,
up to my eyes, ears or throat in.
Believe me, you don't want to know.
When you arrive
it'll become too late to go back.
A conversation of matter, not fact.
Nocturnal, you know I remember everything.
I just don't talk about it.
I just can't feel it
anymore.

You're right, who cares?
I've got the hills of Arizona ahead of me.
The hot high desert
and the lonely low.
The loneliest, at most.

I'm afraid there's not one alley in sight,
no safe place to hide anything.
In other words, I'm afraid.
I can't worship California.
My prayers are like your promises:
written on little slips of paper
and discarded along the highway
every seven and half miles.

In other words, the entire continent
is my kitchen. My
crazy.
And the radio will only play love songs,
in other words:
I can only listen to something about
someone going a million miles away,
but writing a letter every day.

Nocturnal, how many is a million?
How many prayers would that be?

•

I hear you're in the desert. I hear you.
I hear you're sick of mooning
over a conversation that never happened.
I hear you're tired of asking, tired
of—what's the matter? I promise not to ask.

Or maybe just once.
Just one time so I can say,
Morning, you were so right
to scatter, to be with the desert,
to stare at the sun. To get in
tight with the horizon. Hang the blue sky
over the desert.
The desert hides everything.

Morning, you were so right.
You know what I know about California?
California is bored with prayers.
California keeps all the millions of lost
and lonely missives under its pillow. It keeps my promises.
California knows what it's like
to be up to your throat in shit—
California doesn't care.

We've cranked the windows down.
We've done the old-fashioned-
drive-all-night-until-dead-birds-litter-the-highway.
We've worn out all the breakup songs
there are to play. In other words,
we've heard their pitch—

California—what would that take? If offered,
I'd opt for instead, and instead
I'd scoop any semblance of a prim
soul out of my head to keep myself

from singing. Fling its carcass
out a half-cracked window
and let the wind whistle, instead.

Let Otis whistle on into silence.

I'd let momentum take me through
into whatever darkness it should.
In other words, some songs
aren't worth the congealing glue
left on their price tags. Others are.

Whisper a lyric for me, a Joshua tree,
a desert wind to lure me
on. Yes, I've been following you.
Yes, I've been counting trees
back to the crossroads,
to see where they bought souls

with the blues. I asked everyone I saw how long
until the continent slips away. How long
before we can sleep? In prayers? In songs?
They told me a few more.

A very few.

•

I wouldn't believe them.
Believe me, I wouldn't.
I'm here,
not still, but finally,
and I'll tell you what I know already:
these streets ain't narrow.
In fact, they never end.
No one here wears shoes
and there's not a broken bottle in sight.
In other words,
you'll never need your legs again.
Unless you dance.
I can't remember, Nocturnal,
do you dance?

And what I've learned about dead birds?
It's the ol if-you-love-something-set-it-free.
At least that's what I've learned
about garbage.

Everything comes to California to die.
Everything.
It's intoxicating.
It is tectonic.
It's the ol weather's-here-wish-you-were-beautiful.
And never the other way around.
Never.

Everything in sight is either
a postcard or a sad song,
a love letter or a slow dance.
California buries the darkness with the dead.
In other words,
I'm afraid
for you, Nocturnal.

I'm afraid you should
turn yourself
right
around.

It's the ol square-peg-in-a-round....
The old fox with his head caught down the rabbit's hole.

Nocturnal, if you don't die,
you may have to dig your way out.

In other words,
I wouldn't believe them.
Believe me, I wouldn't.

•

Don't worry, I don't
listen. To them or anyone
any more. Believe me like I believe
the next exit
will be the last or
the best.

Oh, Morning. I dig myself
out every day.
And it doesn't mean I'm not dead.
It doesn't mean I've come to believe in handfuls
of daisies tossed on a grave.
It doesn't mean I believe what I've spoken, or heard, or I
can get my head around a love letter.

I believe in blooming, how it comes
from knowing dirt is your bed, even
how it grows from rain and promises—
even mine, with the darkness
of their broken wings

looming. But I see what you mean about garbage.

I see what you mean about not wearing shoes
because we all end up dead,
and anyway. We all end
up in square holes.
I may have been
round to begin with.
Round and round with you. That was before.

Morning, you're still there, or,
if I know you, you're listening
to The Strokes. You're somewhere.
You're in California, so you know.

You know I'm almost,
and been that way as long as either
of us can remember.
But I'm soon, too. And nearly.

It'll be my turn when I get there.
I'll take. Oh, I'll turn.
I'll turn in a slow dance with you
in a rooftop bar. And I'll say this:

all dancing should be slow.

What will we do up there?
From on high. Will we admire bodies
of water by starlight?
Will the river be the same
as it was? I'm afraid
not. What do you think of that?

In other words,
will we watch a single pearl
of condensation glide
down a bottle's neck?
Will we know the difference between?

That will be California,
and I will be later,
I'm afraid. Did I mention that?
Much later than I thought. Because
I'm also afraid to tell the greater truth,
that I'll look towards the water
and call a ditch a ditch.

•

If that's your biggest worry,
I wouldn't.
I wouldn't bother believing in starlight
from any height,
any amount of stairs.

I am staring at the Pacific,
face-to-face.
And believe me, it surrounds.
It will dust off our graves
with one little lick.
It will swallow us whole
whenever it sees fit.

The whole thing about fear
is never knowing.
Never knowing what will happen
when you let go.
When there's no one left
to talk you off the ledge.
It's freedom.
It's a want. Like
driving over Mulholland
only to wish someone's name
into the clouds. Into the sky.
In other words,
it's frightening.

Nocturnal, what would you like
to write in the sky?
What would you like to stitch
in your skin?

Take your time.
No one here is waiting for you.

Always, anymore, or longer.
No one's beating their head
against the wall.
And that's the truth.
The greatest and the worst.
One-step-forward-two-steps-back.
Or is it the other way around?
Which way is it, Nocturnal? You
tell me. I'll

tell you: a shovel won't get you anywhere.
Unless you trade sleeping under the stars for
sleeping under the sea.
Unless you grow gills.
In other words, until you can slit
your own throat.

Can you handle that?

Is it a deal, Nocturnal?
Do we
have a deal?

•

It's a deal.
I'll find a tungsten shovel.
I'll find something designed
for sinking. Every time the sun rises
in California, I'll sleep in the sea.
You can watch me trade
breezes for a wet nap,
for a weed cap in some dark density,
a place away from heat,
away from angry looks and traffic.

The first time I came here I watched
the Pacific.
I sat on a swing and saw the hour when
darkness chased the surfers

out of Hermosa. The chains squeaked.
And everything drowned
in droplets of rose. Now I can't even see
the mountains, even though they're close
enough to lick. The air is viscous,
grey. The early spring days get too long
with all this face to face,
with all this choking.
There's no color left for the sky.

I'd write one word up there,
BLUE, and I'd write it in all
capital letters and I'd write it in
black magic marker. Children
would ask, why does the sky say blue?

We'd say because
it really isn't. We'd say
because it's one step forward

and a backward stagger.
I'd tattoo that on my forehead
with the help of a curb,
a pirouette, and a hard fall.

Morning, the first time
I swaggered into LA
it was dramarama. It was lost angels.
I'd give them anything-anything-anything.
And now?
Well, you know about now.
You know how nothing
terrifies me more than daylight-
savings time. Nothing is worse
than losing a single hour when
it's all you've ever wanted.

You've never been afraid
of now, the way I've been
of after. Of when I'll slit
my other wrist with an amber bottle. Of when I'll bleed.

I'll handle that when night smothers us.
Grace comes easiest in darkness.

I'm stubborn as tequila. And graceless. And I go
straight for the head.
And you should know that well
before we make any kind of deal.

Don't say anything
that bleeding daybreak can't heal, that time can't make
a grave for. In other words,
don't fret. Don't get anxious. The point is—
it's not nearly last call yet.

The point is—
I have half a mind to keep going.

I have half
a roll of quarters, and there's a jukebox
right by the dance floor.
It's right where we left it.

Morning, will you give me
that hour back? You'll see.
I'll only need the one.

•

Nocturnal, I guess
we should talk.
I've fallen for someone,
some thing, else.
No one you know.
No one I know, either.
It was you, but different.
You, but only the way I saw you
in my mind.

The jukebox is gone.
I looked last night.
I watched the moon cut itself in half.
I danced to silence,
swept the dust off the floor
with my feet.

People thought I was crazy, Nocturnal.
Do you think I'm crazy?

Whatever questions we answer out here
will have to be answered honestly.
I can't replenish what hour after hour takes away,
what the ears hear when they've spent too much time
listening to each other every day.

Do you know, Nocturnal?
Do you know, the gulls are loudest right before dawn?
They get nervous.
They get scared they will be stuck staring
at the same stagnant moon
forever.

When you arrive,
I will have already slept with

the sea.
And, no, I won't have extra.
Extra or enough.

The way I see it:
play the game,
or leave the table.
Make your bed,
lie in it.
There's no use pretending there's any other way.
Reap what you sow.
If you can't
handle the heat,
slip into lead shoes
and let go.
Let go.
The way I see it,
it's all one big game,
the ol' over-under strategy.
60/40, 80/20.
In other words, Nocturnal,
when I leave, I'll leave loaded.

In other words,
the way I see it,
you'll have to find it in your heart
to forgive me.
Does it still work that way?
Does it still work?

•

I do think you're crazy,
but we're both
shuffling to the voices in our heads.
I think there's slate under it all.
Maybe it's you. Maybe it's me.
Or fate. You see, I never abandoned the table. I waited for you
to pick up the cue. I kept my left hand on felt.
But you went on waltzing
while I stood in the dark. Morning, I was there.
Whatever you've got, it still works.
I saw the dust coat your toes.

How close to you
did I get last night, swigging that margarita
in some no-name dive in Barstow?
I didn't speak. I had to go. I had to scream
through the heat of the 10
all the way back to Vegas, back
to where I'd been. I had to hide inside.

Everyone thinks I am
a stranger there.

Everyone listens to fountains in parking lots
and it never matters if you're crazy.
No one notices that one of my eyes has gone
hazy, the other hollow, and how smoke follows me
everywhere now. Even without wind.
Want to know something I found?

I found forgiveness in my heart
filed just before forgone.
And the conclusion—

there's always something more.
In other words, there's nothing
for me to forgive.
There was never a lie too deep.
I've known all there is
to know about that, about a him or a her and not getting
to reap what one sows.

I've always been honest with the moon.

The moon is cutting itself in half.
I'm betting. But that's just another game, right?
I hear you about loaded.
Is that the real deal?
You know the real deal scares me. Bad.
You know so much,
I always make my hard decisions
wait for you.

The way I'm
waiting for the time when I'll lean back
from the edge of a building,
lean all the way back and let go
of the line. It's been so long. And coming.

Will you tell me again
what gulls have to say about endings?

•

The edge of the world is
the edge of the world.

Our final day on Earth will be
our final day on Earth.

In other words,
the conclusion may only be
the conclusion.

I was in Nevada the last time I cried.
I saw the desert disappear in a sheet of rain,
the kind of clouds that divide continuously.
It was infinite.

Nocturnal,
I can feel your eyes
burning into the back of my brain.
I can feel it so much sometimes
I can't breathe.

I tried talking to someone today.
Someone I saw on the street.
They said when their hands start to shake
they picture the horizon.
They picture a boat off in the distance
moving with the tide.
They said they sync their breath to its motion.

Do you think that will do the trick?

They told me:
I can always practice forgiveness,
but I will never forget.

Nocturnal, do they really mean never?

I have so much room here.
I have watched the sun
saturate the ocean twelve times and
I am bored with myself.
Bored with my own beauty.

The gulls don't talk but someone did say
you would call my name
when you crossed the California border.
So far, nothing.
So far, I am still fighting with myself,
and as sadness turns to anger,
as another moon eats the day,
this is turning into a real-deal war.

Whatever secrets we share out here
will have to be shared in darkness.

California has the kind of light
that makes everything appear clearly,
as long as you don't look too close and
as long as you never consider hindsight.
I wouldn't play that game anyway.
Poor odds.
It's equal, Nocturnal.
You know, it's 20/20.
All this to say: I do miss you.
All this to say, and no one to speak to.

It takes twelve and a half days
for sadness to turn into anger.
It takes 2.3 seconds to fall from a ledge,

to come to a conclusion.
Like I said, Nocturnal,
this is surely the slowest death.

•

Save something.
Save the last dance
for the last day.
We were always promised that, weren't we?
We were always promised a chance. But
I forget by whom I never forget when—
I know you remember, too,
remember it's when-hell-freezes-over.
Those 2.3 seconds when the day closes and the world ceases
to turn.

That's when they said the pull
of a full moon would finally be enough
for us both. It will be.

It will be blue and finally. It will be an eclipse
as perfect as any polished skull. That's my conclusion.
It will be open, and it will have a jagged hole
in its back for hindsight, for a soul to get out,
for air.

That's my conclusion.

A movement to sigh
is just as easily a movement
to speak. It gives purpose
to the hollow in your chest.

I talked to someone, too.
I hummed an M.
I did my best. I exhaled sound carved
into the shape of an O. I swallowed it.
I let my lips sink into I,
when no one responded. Alone and so easy.

The trick with I is not to smile, to sync
your tears with the truth.

The truth is, I say your name every time the sun rises.

The truth is,
the gulls aren't talking because they have nothing
nice to say. So far. The truth is,
there's nothing nice to say about Nevada, either.
The rain poured into a fissure in the desert.
It was infinite, but it still just disappeared.

Never is sooner, and tighter, than you think.

Now the sun bends around a red
outcrop of stone, and its top
has flared into smoke and embers.
At the edge of the world
even the rocks catch fire.

The horizon never helped me when
my hands started to shake, when I missed you enough
to chew through my own cheek.
The horizon never helped me
at all. That weak curve only showed me
what served to separate
you from me. And still does.

Sparks fade in cold air.

Get eaten by clouds.
Flicker less with every moment
spent away from fuel.

In other words, for once I'd love
that luxury.
I'd love to be bored
with beauty.

•

You know, Nocturnal, it is all about fire.
That's exactly what it boils down to;
some thing to prove we are all
equally insignificant.

Look, I want to be honest;
I appreciate your distance:
as long as the horizon, and thicker.

Today is the second day I've seen a dead fox on the road.
I only look long enough to recognize its face,
to come to that conclusion.

Nocturnal, do you believe when it's over, it's over?
Do you believe some things just run their course?

I will never need you.
I think you know that.
I think you know
I know
you're smarter than me.
I think I'm right.
I think.
But speculation only detracts from concentration.
Like chasing your own tail:
blink your eyes and you're bound
to get hit.

I've been hollow and heavy
at the same time.
I've been impossible.
In other words, Nocturnal,
your distance takes the monkey right off my back.
Right off.

Look, I want to die honest
and alone.
I want to get on the freeway,
say goodbye to the sea,
close my eyes and let my car drive itself
right into downtown.
Right in.

Nocturnal, do you expect me to keep
falling and falling for everything else?
Everything except you?

Last night I fell asleep
listening to a song that said something like:
it ain't natural to cry in the midnight.
It's about a girl dying of a disease.
A real-deal disease.
That, or a broken heart,
a broken head.
It's hard to tell which.

Look, I've become dangerous.

I think I would be better off
to kick the habit,
to let you go.
And that's not frightening
anymore.
But the disease is.
The after effect.
The after the fact.
The midnight.

It ain't natural.

That's exactly what it boils down to, Nocturnal.

What else do you expect me to do?

•

Morning, you're absolutely
right about it. Sometimes the fox isn't
stupid. Sometimes he just wants
to get hit.
Just once or twice, by separating
headlights. Two as one.
So perfect. So instant. So round.

You know I don't sleep,
lying down or otherwise.
You know I don't believe
a circle is ever over.
I don't believe we can say that.
I believe it like I believe
in the orbits of bodies.
It's impossible to separate them.

Just once or twice I'd like this:
to hear you gasp from hope,
to hear something new from you, anything
instead of that single hiss of resignation.
That never, that tire punctured by a mess of screws.

I may be far away,
but I know where the city is dying.
I know what from.
It's from blinking lights and chasing
tails. I know there's no place better
to be dangerous, no place
better to play in traffic.
In other words, there's no place
more significant.
Right or wrong. Short, long,
or indifferent. Home.

We stash the road away
every time we drive it,
rolling it up like the last carpet
that ever got stained with blood.
It's gone.
Behind us

the fox may be lolling
its tongue across the yellow line,
it may have a fly
where I should be. A clot.
A little one.

Throw us all on a pyre, all and each.
Let the ash float away
on the Santa Ana wind.

Let the world return to smoke.
The world has a habit of smoking.

One day you'll let it all go away
with the end of the last song in your stereo,
and one day, when you least expect it—
in other words, one day when you're least—
you'll stand in the dark and a fresh flash of dusk-red
will light your mirror.

I may be smart.
I may be the fine monkey or
the clever fox.
On your back. Or closer. As ever.
Pirouette away from the sun as it rises
and I'll tell you a secret through the peephole
we drilled in your skull. Through your fever.

I'm immediately.
I'm there, in front of you,
letting the waves wash over my head.
I've always been

letting it all
go over
my head.

I expect you to go,
like you always go.
Downtown,
toward the howl of ambulances.
Toward the canned laughter or away
from care. Kick me if I'm sleeping. I expect I'll follow.
Hell, I expect I'm already there,

dying. There's nothing more natural.

•

It's 12:01, Nocturnal.
It's tomorrow already.

You don't know this but
in the thick of downtown
there's too much noise
to hear anything.
It's filtered, filthy,
otherwise.

I'm not going to say one thing about us.
Faith is like fire, a four-letter word.
And I've been counting.
I've become good
again.

Is that what you were hoping to hear?
Once or repeated,
I said, is that what you were hoping to hear?

This is the finest I've felt, lost.
It's an easy decision,
I follow the one-way streets,
and everything is alive
because nothing else can exist:
no moonlight to dance in,
no shadows to chase.
It's always straight as an arrow,
always on the way to a dead end.

But I am not going to say a thing about you.
Wherever you think you are, you aren't.
I don't mean that mean,
I just mean it.
I wouldn't kick you if I could.

I wouldn't start something I couldn't stop.
Ever.

If you're here,
I'll be back by the Pacific tomorrow.
Pick a time and place.
Pick your favorite song on the jukebox.
Pick your feet out of the darkness
and show your tired face.
Once, or twice, or wait, just once:
for the first time.

Nocturnal, do you remember the first time?
I don't, and I've been counting.
Every notch is another hole in the head, the heart,
mine or yours,
doesn't matter.

I hate to sound like a broken record,
but it never ever did.
It never ever did too much for me, Nocturnal.

But I'm not going to say another thing about us,
like that.
What's that saying:
fake it till you make it?
Half of life is just showing up?
Same thing, as far as I'm concerned.
Same exact thing.

I suggest you arrive early,
have a cocktail waiting for me.
Choose a pretty place,
something with a view.
Somewhere I can walk to the water

and throw my feet in the waves.
Pretend you're trying to impress me.

I'll buy it
because I want to,
because, unfortunately,
we are not going to die tomorrow,
or today.
Same exact thing.
As far as, and filthier.

I suggest you wear red or blue.
Wear it like a stranger.
I hate to say it,
but I like you best that way.
And I don't mean that mean,
I just mean it.

•

Morning, I'm good, too. I'm better than hoping
for turns off a one-way street.
Ruts or alleys. Broken
records never did much
for me, either. I like to improvise too much. I like so —.
Let's exist
just to be contrary.
You and I have no stomach for rules.

Go wherever you want. Jump the groove.
I mean it. Just go. Feel yourself unspool.
Go wherever. Go tomorrow.
Fill your pockets with all
the letters I sent, a rough stone,
and a wooden match. Spin into that
scent of seaweed and diesel at the first
joint you find. The one on the point.

You remember the first.
You remember time.

I like to think of you as that corner,
in that instant a table by a neglected tree.
Dryer and thirstier than I've ever been. More able.

Sit down. Let our distance ignite.
Think "jukebox." And "fever."

I'll be there.
I just wanted to hear you say it.
I just wanted you to prefer me
stranger. I just wanted an excuse to switch myself
for someone made of shadows. Someone less known.

Look around.

I'll be the one in filthy red. I'll be now.
I'll be the one with whiskey, neat.
I'll be your lever against loneliness. And if not then, you might
try the sunset after.
And if not after, then anew.
I've been training for a blue sky.
Soon I'll be ready for flight.

FOUR

The Table

We'll walk out.

Yes.

*Morning, our fate will bear down on us
like forever, like until, like never, like every
minute before or since piled onto our chests.*

Until never turns into now. Until always slowly blurs into when.

But.

Until then, we'll share what we can.

*After the fox, after even the best dancing
and streetlights, after the fog of the too-much-
brandy and the not-enough-not-ever-enough,
it will still be tomorrow.*

Whatever words come sliding
out our crooked mouths.

*After your face in the doorway. After your joke.
When the sun drags its lame red leg
out of the ocean, it will make silhouettes a certainty.*

Whatever words we'd like to take back.
Not south, but surely gone.
There's a table somewhere.

It will limp past the locked doors, past the black ones,

There's a chance to stop.

past the blue, past the gloom of wooden mouths
cut into the front of every building,

Or to keep going.

past a certain point. Yes, gone.
Past figures that blurred.

To keep banging our heads against a brick wall.

Past goodbye, now. Past how.

To carry on laughing.

Past the bus stop with so many angry
faces looming like trench-coat trees, past coping,
past hope of we, past fate. Past our alley again.

Yes, there's a table somewhere.

Past the bloated eight-o'clock train. Past mine.
And just past suddenly.

There is a table.

You'll shine, hurrying away or toward.

I'll probably turn to you, say:
"Trust me from here forward,
from here till tomorrow, till now."
I'll probably mean it. I'll probably run
through the streets like it was July,
like there was never a need
for goodbye, like there was never a need.

And I will see you there, behind the others.
All of them lit by you.

At all.

Just the contours of you, just the crumbs
you throw to the crying birds.

After facing the fate of after, after anything,
after is just a million minutes away from before.

But it will be you all the same,
your ways, and same as always.

So before I see you, practice.
Practice saying something you do mean.

In other words, I figure I will keep on
going. In other words, so will you.

Practice how it feels after that. In other words, feel that.
That after. That one-in-a-million minute.

Until.

I know.
I will always be all the same.
I know. I've seen the fox at dawn.
There, chasing its tail. I know.
There's a chance to stop,
and there's a chance to keep going.

Acknowledgments

The authors would like to thank the following online and print journals for publishing sections from *After the Fox:*

Pacific (Sections 1-6) in *In Stereo* (instereopress.com)

Morning, you're in it; *We could be anywhere,* and *Watching is serious* in *Otoliths*

How simple would it be to replace light and *How simple would it be to replace you* in *E-Ratio*

I hear you're in the desert. I hear you.; *I wouldn't believe them*; *Don't worry, I don't*; *If that's your biggest worry,* and *It's a deal* in *Cricket Online Review*

I anticipated you would say that and *Anticipate me at the end* in *Grist*

After the fox, see in *Ink Node*

You know, Nocturnal, it is all about fire; *Morning you're absolutely*; *It's 12:01, Nocturnal,* and *Morning, I'm good, too. I'm better than hoping* forthcoming in *Moria.*

Finally, thanks to Black Lawrence Press for featuring some of these poems on their website for the 2011 and 2014 National Poetry Month spotlight series.

Travis Cebula writes, teaches, and publishes in Colorado. He earned an MFA in 2009 from Naropa University, the same year he founded Shadow Mountain Press. He is the author of six chapbooks and four full-length collections of poetry, including *... but for a Brief Interlude at Versailles, Ithaca, One Year in a Paper Cinema,* and *After the Fox.* You can find him in Paris every summer teaching with the Left Bank Writers Retreat.

Sarah Suzor's full-length collection of poetry, *The Principle Agent,* won the 2010 Hudson Prize, and was published by Black Lawrence Press in 2011. She is also the author of multiple chapbooks including *It was the season, then.* (EtherDome Chapbooks) and *Isle of Dogs* (Toadlily Press). Her poetry can be found in various online and print journals as well as anthologized and translated. *After the Fox* (Black Lawrence Press) is her most current release, and a collaborative effort with Travis Cebula. Suzor was born in Sheridan, WY, but resides in Venice, CA. She also teaches creative writing workshops throughout the states, and at the Left Bank Writers Retreat in Paris, France.